Marjorie E. Favretto, in her retirement years, lives in her native Nova Scotia with her husband, Reno. She wrote her first book of poetry at age 40 for her graduating nursing class, emphasizing "the person in the patient." This collection of poems was often used as a teaching tool in schools of nursing in the USA, Australia, New Zealand, and Great Britain.

Through *Avatars of the Ages*, she offers her readers "her tiny flame in the great candelabra of the world."

To the Eternal Flame: the source of my inspiration; and to Reno, whose spirit lifts mine in that quiet space.

Marjorie E. Favretto

AVATARS OF THE AGES

Timeless Words

AUSTIN MACAULEY PUBLISHERS™
LONDON · CAMBRIDGE · NEW YORK · SHARJAH

Copyright © Marjorie E. Favretto (2019)

All rights reserved. No part of this publication may be reproduced, distributed, or transmitted in any form or by any means, including photocopying, recording, or other electronic or mechanical methods, without the prior written permission of the publisher, except in the case of brief quotations embodied in critical reviews and certain other non-commercial uses permitted by copyright law. For permission requests, write to the publisher.

Any person who commits any unauthorized act in relation to this publication may be liable to criminal prosecution and civil claims for damages

Ordering Information:
Quantity sales: special discounts are available on quantity purchases by corporations, associations, and others. For details, contact the publisher at the address below.

Publisher's Cataloging-in-Publication data
Favretto, Marjorie E.
Avatars of the Ages: Timeless Words

ISBN 9781645362784 (Paperback)
ISBN 9781645362777 (Hardback)
ISBN 9781645368717 (ePub e-book)

Library of Congress Control Number: 2019911796

The main category of the book — POETRY / Subjects & Themes / Inspirational & Religious

www.austinmacauley.com/us

First Published (2019)
Austin Macauley Publishers LLC
40 Wall Street, 28th Floor
New York, NY 10005
USA

mail-usa@austinmacauley.com
+1 (646) 5125767

Table of Contents

Preface	**13**
Words of Love	**15**
Beyond Forever	*17*
Amen	*18*
Best Wishes	*19*
Hi There!	*20*
The Bench	*21*
I Love You	*22*
Lost Years	*23*
The Latest Word	*24*
Dance On	*25*
The Keepsake	*26*
If Only	*27*
Mommy	*28*
Blessed by Love	*29*
Puppy Love	*30*

Gramma's Day	*31*
Togetherness	*32*
The Mirror	*33*
Knowing	*34*
Words of Praise	**35**
Heartbeat	*37*
Soul Dance	*38*
The News	*39*
Simple Things	*40*
Angels	*41*
My Imagination	*42*
Did I?	*43*
Legacy	*44*
Words of Kindness	**45**
The Thief	*47*
How Are You?	*48*
Silence	*49*
The Playground	*50*
I Was Going To	*51*
Blinded Eyes	*52*
One of These Days	*53*
Full Circle	*54*
Regeneration	*55*

Words of Faith   **57**

You Are Not Alone   59

Believe   60

The Vault   61

The Good Book   62

The Potter   63

Not-So-Faraway Land   64

Trial Run   65

The Melody   66

Carpe Diem   67

Words of Hope   **69**

Hi Daddy   71

Hope   72

Awakening   73

The Promise   74

Providence   75

The Way   76

Estrangement   77

Therapy Sessions   78

Words of Gratitude   **79**

The Quest   81

Gratitude   82

Small Town Boys   83

Alive, Alive, Oh!	*84*
Blessed Am I	*85*
Gems	*86*
Forever Young	*87*
Tomorrow?	*88*
Words of Trust	**89**
Let It Be	*91*
Run, Run, Run	*92*
My Collection	*93*
Be Still	*94*
On Course	*95*
Inspiration	*96*
Have We Met?	*97*
Solace	*98*
Maybe	*99*
Forgiveness	*100*
Words of Peace	**101**
Utopia	*103*
Peace	*104*
Celebration	*105*
Serenity	*106*
Hey God!	*107*
Downtime	*108*

A Better 'Me'	*109*
Reverie	*110*
Words to Ponder	**111**
The Carpenter	*113*
Chasing the Dream	*114*
Temptation	*115*
Poor Rich Man	*116*
Party Time	*117*
The Game of Life	*118*
Golden Years	*119*
The Gate	*120*
The Sea of Life	*121*
Remember?	*122*
Drumming	*123*
The Answer	*124*
Just 'Be There'	*125*
Reality	*126*
Voices of Nature	**127**
Awesome!	*129*
Spring	*130*
Summer	*131*
Welcome	*132*
Country Lane	*133*

Beside the Sea	*134*
R.S.V.P.	*135*
Winter Beauty	*136*
Mountain Majesty	*137*
Seasons	*138*
God's Healing Balm	*139*
Celestial Colors	*140*
Marjorie-isms	**141**

Preface

So many different messages are conveyed in the words,
"I love you!"
So, too,
in the words of the cosmic poets;
their voices heard
in countless different ways.
In these verses, I record for you the messages I receive
as I reflect on their written word.
What message will you hear?

— Marjorie E. Favretto

Words of Love

Beyond Forever

Psalm 108:4—For great is Your love, O Lord,
higher than the heavens.

Beyond what eyes have ever seen,
beyond what ears have heard,
beyond all thoughts that one can dream,
beyond the telling in mere words.

Beyond the earth,
the skies, the sun,
higher than the heavens.
The nameless breath
in everyone,
Love!
Beyond forever!

Amen

*Co 3:17—Whatever you do in word or deed,
do all in the name of the Lord.*

*Hands of the surgeon mending the heart;
Hands of the painter creating his art.
Hands of the carpenter building homes;
Hands of the poet writing poems.
Hands of the farmer in fields sowing seeds;
Hands of the fisherman gnarled by the seas.*

*Hands of the father guiding his son;
Hands of the soldier grasping his gun.
Hands of the mother tending babies' needs.*

*Hands of the old folk in pews, praying beads.
Hands of women, hands of men
blessing us with their Amen!*

Best Wishes

*Lao Tzu—If you wish to possess something,
you must first give it away.*

*May your life be strewn
with the tiniest of pebbles;
no boulders to shoulder,
no mountains to cross over.
More sunshine than rain,
more wellness than pain.
Less enemies than friends;
more wealth
than you can spend.*

*And above all,
Love.
Love without end.*

Hi There!

*Dalai Lama—Love and Compassion are necessities;
without them humanity cannot survive.*

> *Just fifteen when touched
> by the footage he had seen
> of war-ravaged lands,
> he vowed to lend a hand.
> Sad little faces fresh in his mind,
> he wanted no child left behind.
> Packing little boxes from that day on;
> yo-yos, flip-flops, and candy bars,
> he sent along those treats and toys
> to orphaned little girls and boys.*

*Just nineteen when he was shot down,
his parachute landing in a war-zone town.
Dazed when he awoke to an orphan's face
gazing at him without a trace of fear.*

> *"Hi there!" she said (little
> flip-flops on her feet). "Do you
> want something to eat?
> Did you come from far?
> I have a yo-yo and a candy bar!"*

The Bench

1 Cor 13:8—Love never ends; all else will pass away.

Pushing her walker, she ambles along,
passing the fountains to the pond;
one thing on her mind...
to find the bench.
She sits and smiles as she remembers
the curly haired little girl
standing on this very bench,
captivated by the swans;
her mother's arms
wrapped around her tiny waist.
Pure joy on her face.
Then she remembers
The curly haired teenage girl
sitting on this very bench,
enchanted by the swans;
her lover's arms
wrapped around her slender waist.
Pure joy on her face.

With tear-filled eyes, she whispers anew
the vow they made to never part;
just before they carved two hearts.
Tracing the etching with wrinkled fingers,
sweet memories linger...

I Love You

John 13:34—Just as I have loved you, so you must love one another.

*It's all the little things you do
that make me love you…
In your touch, in your smile,
though not a word is spoken,
I hear you say, "I love you."
It's all the times you try so hard
to make me laugh, to make me proud;
the secret wink across the room,
the phone call or the tweet at noon
just to say, "I love you."*

*It's all the little things you do
that let me know that
I am loved
as I love you!*

Lost Years

Rumi—Lovers don't finally meet somewhere;
they're in each other all along.

College teens when they met one night.
She was black, he was white;
the world was strange.
They talked, they laughed,
they shared, they cared;
they ran before they dared
fall in love.

A widow and a widower met one night.
She was still black, he still white;
the world had changed.
They talked, they cried,
they shared, they cared;
they kissed and dared
to fall in love.

The Latest Word

*Cor 3:14—Above all be clothed in love,
which binds all things together.*

*In days of yore,
a tooth for a tooth
The latest "Word,"
a different truth.
Be kind to each other,
love without end;
your brother, your neighbor,
your enemy, your friend.*

*Often times, not an easy task
But Love is truly
all God asks.*

Dance On

Jer.1:5—Before I formed you in the womb, I knew you.

*The sculpture,
knocked from the pedestal
just before the final touch;
the unfinished symphony,
never to be heard...
the stillborn child.*

*The beauty, the melody
forever loved,
forever played
in a mother's heart.*

*The Dance goes on
and on
and on...*

The Keepsake

Kahlil Gibran: Love knows not its own depth,
until the hour of separation.

They found it perfectly intact
the day she passed away,
with all the letters he had written
and sent to her each day.
Neatly stored in her cedar chest
for more than fifty years;
every time she looked at it,
her eyes would fill with tears.
Their wedding day was planned
the day he came back from the war.
Instead, news unmistakable
with the knock on her front door.

No one in the family
ever knew the pain she bore,
gazing at her wedding dress;
the one she never wore.

If Only

Rom. 12:9—Love one another with mutual affection.

*If only we could see
into each other's soul,
we'd realize
how very much alike
we've been created.
There'd be no room
for hatred.*

*Hating a little:
much too much.
Loving a little:
not nearly enough!*

Mommy

Luke 18:16—Suffer the little children to come unto me.

She came to see me daddy
in the middle of the night.
When I woke up,
my room was filled
with beautiful bright light!

She smiled at me and held me,
said she loved me more than ever;
she promised me she'd care for me
always, till forever!

Daddy, I'm only seven.
Why did Mommy go back to heaven?

Didn't God have enough angels?

Blessed by Love

Psalm 48:9—I ponder Your steadfast love, O Lord.

> *In a call from a friend*
> *out of the blue,*
> *just to say*
> *'I was thinking of you,'*
> *I feel love.*
>
> *In a waterfall,*
> *birds that fly in an azure sky,*
> *a walk in the woods,*
> *a butterfly,*
> *I touch love.*
>
> *In the eyes of my beloved,*
> *his tender embrace,*
> *I know love!*

Puppy Love

Psalm 34:18—The Lord is near to the brokenhearted.

The first day they met,
they formed a bond;
their love for each other
went beyond anything
she could ever
have imagined.
And the day he died
oh, how she cried
and cried and cried.

He was her constant.
He was her friend.
He was her beloved
rescue puppy.

Gramma's Day

*Col. 3:19—Clothe yourself with love
which binds all things together.*

*In Gramma's day,
a bowl of soup was the cure
for the winter flu.
And "store-bought"
was the rarest of treats;
hand-me-downs were all they knew.
In Gramma's day,
young mothers gave birth
in their own bed;
up and about the very next day
doing the chores and baking bread.
In Gramma's day,
the country doc stopped in
if passing by
to check up on the family,
share tea and homemade pie.
In Gramma's day,
they had precious little;
their needs were very small.
But they had love,
they had it all;
so Gramma says!*

Togetherness

*Rumi—For those who love with heart and soul,
there is no such thing as separation.*

*In the winter of his life,
he remembers the summers,
he remembers the springs
and all the wonderful things
they shared together.
He remembers their travels
and places they've been.
He remembers the good times
and the many times when
they laughed together.
He remembers how often
he said, "I love you."
He remembers she said,
"I love you too,"
when they loved together.
In the winter of his life,
all his "remembers"
are all their "togethers"
now that she's passed on.*

The Mirror

Lao Tzu—When I let go of what I am, I become what I might be.

*While seated at the opera house
in your jewel-encrusted gown,
do you ever think of the tenements
on the other side of town?*

*While your dinners are always
a four-course fare,
do you assure the "hungry"
have their share?
Is your wardrobe labeled
"designer wear,"
while others go naked?
Do you care?*

*When you look into the mirror,
Is Love reflected back at you,
or is there something you should do
to change your image?*

Knowing

Buddha—When you like a flower, you pluck it.
When you love a flower, you water it.

As through a field of daisies,
our path in life meanders.
We pluck the petals
and pose the question:
"He loves me, he loves me not?"

And one beautiful day,
we come upon a rose,
blooming.
Its petals we caress;
our question's been addressed.

We know!

Words of Praise

Heartbeat

Psalm 96:1—O sing to the Lord a new song;
sing to the Lord, all the earth.

In every heart, there beats a song.
Celtic and folk across the lands,
opera, classical, the world's big bands.
Beating of the native drums,
Christmas' pum rum pum pums.

Pop, hip-hop, jazz, and the blues;
Spiritual chanting in Sunday pews.
Toe-tappin', hand clappin'
guitar strummin' sing-alongs.
In every heart, there beats a song.

I'm listening for yours;
do you
hear mine?

Soul Dance

Ephes 5:19—Sing and make melody to the Lord with your heart.

Love stirs the rhythm
in my veins that
plays the music
in my heart,
to which my soul
dances!

The News

*Psalm 139:14—O God, I praise You,
for I am fearfully and wonderfully created.*

*I decided last night,
the time is right
to break the news.
I've got nothing to lose…
except my family;
God help me!*

*Perhaps they already know;
I don't think so…*

*Mom, Dad, I'm going to marry
Larry.*

Congratulations, son!

Simple Things

Psalm 66:1—Make a joyful noise to God, all the earth.

Joy is found in the simple things:
seashells, snowflakes, butterfly wings.
Building castles in the sand,
strolling the boardwalk hand in hand.
Children cartwheeling on the lawn,
little girls trying dad's shoes on.
Singing in the shower
to your heart's delight,
sharing dinner by candlelight.

Painted faces at the fair,
riding a roller coaster on a dare.
Tracing pictures in the clouds,
dancing with abandon in a crowd.
Acting young no matter your age,
always eager to turn the page.
Open to whatever tomorrow may bring;

find your joy in the simple things.

Angels

Psalm 91:11—He will command His angels to guard you.

*Ordained by God to be our guide
Angels, ever at our side.
Our praise and thanks
and all our needs to
God they bring upon
their wings.*

*Faithful guardians
in pain and strife,
embrace them,
welcome them into your life.
Angels unfailing
day and night;
they dwell in Love,
they live in the Light.*

My Imagination

1 Chron 28:9—If you seek Him, He will let you find Him.

*I'd never know the beauty
that lies beneath the sea,
the view from the highest mountain
or the joy that there could be
if everyone loved their neighbor
and all the world was free;*

*if it weren't for
my imagination!*

Did I?

*Psalm 42:8—At night, His song is ever with me;
a prayer to the God of my life.*

*At the end of the day,
did I remember to be kind?
Did I stimulate my mind?
Did I tend to my body?
Did I hurt anybody?
Did I learn any lessons?
Did I give thanks for my blessings?
Did I respond to God's grace?
Did I make the world a better place?
Did I serve the Lord?
Did I keep His word?
Did I pray, did I play,
or did I miss the chance
to celebrate the Dance?*

Legacy

*Buddha—Three things cannot be hidden:
the sun, the moon, and the truth.*

*The sun coming up each morning,
the moon rising high above,
gardens blooming in the spring
the magic of falling in love.*

*The bees that pollinate the fields,
the lakes sustained by rain,
the perfect rhythm of the heart,
the wonder of our brain.*

*Perhaps we'll never walk
through the parting of the sea;
our miracle is Truth itself,
Providential legacy.*

Words of Kindness

The Thief

*Dalai Lama—Open your arms to change
but never let go of loving kindness.*

*My "Mrs." is full of joy and life;
this woman I visit is not my wife!
My "Mrs." never has a hair out of place;
this woman needs help to wash her face.
My "Mrs." loves to host lavish affairs;
this woman just sits in her room and stares.
My "Mrs." keeps a beautiful home;
this woman just wants to be left alone.*

*I never met this woman before in my life!
Dementia,
where have you hidden my wife?*

How Are You?

Khalil Gibran—Tenderness and kindness are not signs of weakness but manifestations of strength.

When we ask a friend, "How are you?"
do we really want
an answer?
Do we really want to hear
about their worries and their fears;
how they soaked the pillow
through the night
with their never-ending tears?
Do we want to let them tell us
they've been diagnosed with cancer;
that they've just been laid off work
and they don't have any answers?
Do we really take the time to see
behind their frozen smiles?

Are we prepared to walk with them
a hundred fear-filled miles?
Or do we ask, "How are you?"
and just hope
that they don't answer!

Silence

Prov. 16:24—Pleasant words as honeycomb; sweet to the soul.

*Silence is more
than the absence of sound.
In the depths of depression
with ado all around,
there's a silence.
Not understanding
the cards they've been dealt,
they long to be part of the joy
they once felt before
the silence.*

*Stand not idly by.
With love we must try
to speak to their heart
in their silence.*

The Playground

Luke 6:31—Do unto others as you would have them do unto you.

*Don't hate me
because I have dark skin;
this is the skin I was born in.
Don't hate me
because I cannot run.
I wear a brace; it isn't fun.
Don't hate me
because my mom's your maid;
I have no dad,
I wish I had.
Don't hate me
because I have no lunch;
share yours.
Don't hate me
because I have no friends;
be one!*

*Don't hate me.
It hurts me.*

I Was Going To

Gandhi—Happiness is when what you think, what you say and what you do are in harmony.

I was going to send you a card,
but I forgot the day.
I was going to pay you a visit,
but then you moved away.
I was going to say, "I'm sorry,"
I meant to…yesterday.

I was going to tell you
"I love you."
Alas, you passed away.

I was going to…

Blinded Eyes

Dalai Lama—Be kind whenever possible; it is always possible!

*Do we deem a man worthless
If he's clad in tattered rags?
Do we really believe the richest man
is the one with the
moneybags?*

*Sadly for us, too much of the time
we see with blinded eyes.
When we meet the man in the rags,
we simply pass him by.*

*We judge by his clothes
and set him apart,
missing the goodness
that lives in his heart.
His treasure known
to God alone.*

One of These Days

Gandhi—Be the change you want to see in the world.

*With the world-wide web
we've come so far,
yet do any of us know
who our neighbors are?
Is the nod of the head
the best we can give?
Such an empty way to live!*

*Day after day, the same routine;
no time for living, so it seems.
I intend to change that
one of these days,
one of these years…
I tell myself, but
'Myself' doesn't hear!*

Full Circle

*Lao Tzu—Life and death are one thread;
the same line viewed from different ends.*

> *I held fast to my mother's hand
> when I was afraid,
> when I was nine.
> It took my fears away.*
>
> *I hold fast to my mother's hand
> when she is afraid,
> now that she's ninety.*
>
> *It takes her fears away,
> I pray!*

Regeneration

*Muhammad—Whoever is deprived of kindness,
is deprived of all good.*

*Wake up people;
don't sleep while we go hungry.
Wake up people;
share with us your country.
Vast tracts of land yet to be tilled;
we come to your borders,
we come with our skills.*

*We come with our children,
we come with our dreams.
We ask for refuge;
we have no schemes
to harm your nation.
We are the generation
of your future.
Wake up, people.*

Words of Faith

You Are Not Alone

James 4:8—Draw nigh to God and He will draw nigh to you.

When you feel your world is crashing down
and the earth is shaky
beneath your feet,
the cliffs too high,
impossible to climb,
take each day one step at a time.
You are not alone.

Extend your hand,
let God be your guide.
He'll lift you up that mountainside.
Dare to put your faith in the Lord;
a rougher road, He trod before.
A heavier load as well, He bore.
You are not alone.

Believe

Psalm 3:5—Trust the Lord with all your heart.

*Inhale the blessings
of this new day;
exhale the worries
of yesterday.*

*God holds the answers
to our needs.
We have His ear
before we plead;
His hand extended,
our burdens to relieve.
Believe!*

The Vault

Psalm 16:6—Indeed I have a good heritage.

*There is a vault in heaven
that opens with a master key.
On the day that we were born,
it was assigned to you and me.
This vault is filled with treasure:
hope and peace and joy and love,
patience, kindness, and well-being;
endless gifts from God above.
These riches are our heritage,
we can draw on the reserve.
It simply takes an act of faith
to believe that we deserve.*

*Let's put aside all trace of pride
and get down on our knees.
Scripture says,
"What's Mine is yours,"
we simply must believe.*

The Good Book

*Prov. 3:6—In all ways acknowledge Him
and He will direct your path.*

*With our birth
comes a detailed map,
we seldom take the time to read;
always searching a better route
to find our truth.*

*We venture down a different path
than the one designed by
the Master Mapmaker.
Alas, losing our way
day after day
to end up God knows where,
when all we really had to do
was read the map!*

The Potter

Jer.18—As clay in the potter's hand, so are you in My hand.

*With every repentant move of our heart,
every embrace of God's will,
a threadlike fissure
weaves its way
through our set and molded clay.*

*Our shards reshaped
by the Divine Potter's hand;
a vessel of beauty now in place
filled with kindness,
love and grace.*

*Pour forth God bids,
your sacred treasure
to all the world
in fullest measure.*

Not-So-Faraway Land

Lao Tzu—At the center of your being, you know who you are and you know what you want.

> *Daydreams took me as a child*
> *to faraway lands;*
> *to places way beyond the sky,*
> *where angels sang.*
> *They could fly;*
> *so could I!*

Childhood, a mere memory now,
those places way beyond the sky
seem not so far away, somehow.

> *I still believe*
> *I can fly!*

Trial Run

Muhammad—The cure for ignorance is to question.

I've seen life prolonged on breathing tubes;
skid row cradling bottles of booze.
I've seen teenagers doping behind schools;
paraplegic therapy in the swimming pool.
I've seen soldiers returning in flag-draped caskets
their families left to wonder
how they can get past this.
I've seen migrant camps; children too weak to cry
while affluent nations turn a blind eye.
I've seen too many mass shootings
where dozens lay dying,
too often because they were simply trying
to worship their God.

In all these trials, I seek God's face.
I probe the meaning of His grace.
One thing I know,
I know nothing, for sure!
Intrinsically I know
we have to do more
to care for each other.

The Melody

Lao Tzu—Music in the soul, can be heard in the universe.

*As Heaven writes its music score,
selected notes are we;
God calls us forth purposely,
to aspire to become
His Melody!*

Carpe Diem

Luke 12: Strive for God's kingdom; all else will be given you.

*Never enough hours in the day;
everything pulling us,
every which way.
The daily bustle, the constant hustle
obscures any semblance of bliss.
Surely, something's amiss...*

*Let's seize the moment
we are in; carpe diem.
Carpe diem!*

Words of Hope

Hi Daddy

*Matt 18:19—Where two of you on earth agree,
so it shall be done by my Father.*

*Our precious child in a coma
fighting for her life;
'round-the-clock vigil
for me and my wife.
Pleading to her angels,
our hopes drowned in fears;
"Please ask God to heal her,"
we prayed through our tears.*

*Three weeks by her bedside
resigned to her dying
when a wee voice from her bed
said,
"Daddy, why are you crying?"*

Hope

Psalm 23:4—Tho' I walk through a dark valley
I fear no evil.

Just when I thought I lost you
I sensed you lurking
in the corners of my heart,
murmuring ever so faintly
to penetrate my despair.
And somewhere
deep inside,
I recognized you.

Your name
is Hope!

Awakening

*Buddha—Just as a candle cannot burn without fire;
man cannot live without a spiritual life.*

*No real purpose, no true focus,
racing here, racing there,
helter skelter like a hare;
seldom finding time
for prayer.*

*Till caught in the grasp
of the Eagle's talons,
my world is shaken;*

I awaken!

The Promise

*1 Sam 16:7—Man sees the outward appearance;
God looks on the heart.*

*A place on the pedestal,
our daily quest.
Our lifetime ambition:
to be the best.
Best in show, best leading man,
best recipe, best vitamin,
best book, best new look,
best car by far.*

*Keep faith, God will honor
our efforts on earth;
remember His promise,
"The last shall be first."*

Providence

*Deut.31:6—Be strong and of good courage;
the Lord will not fail you.*

*Somehow when we're down,
we find the strength to rise.
Somehow in the darkness,
we catch a glimpse of light.*

*Somehow
when we've lost all hope,
we find the grace to cope;*

Somehow...

The Way

John 14:6—I am the Way, the Truth, and the Life.

Huddled under worn-out blankets,
lying on a sidewalk grate;
how did I meet this terrible fate?
In fingerless mittens
clinging to a beggar's cup,
praying strangers fill it up
so I can eat today.
How did I go from designer suits
and custom-made shoes,
to a brown paper bag
'round a bottle of booze?
Success in life before I was a user;
now a degenerate, a loser, alone.

A passerby drops me a coin;
he says, "God bless you, son."
A ray of hope; I am His son!
I'll find the way
back up again!

Estrangement

Omar Khayyam—A hair divides what is false and what is true.

*Tears fell like raindrops
the day her mother died;
the day she lost her daughter,
a river she cried.
Parental rejection,
grief deeper than death;
an ache in her heart
with every breath.*

*Days turn to years;
the pain
does not ease.
Hope stays alive
because she believes
"Mother Love" is eternal;
again they will meet…
United in love,
reunion sweet!*

Therapy Sessions

*Matt 5:3—Blessed are the poor in spirit,
theirs is the kingdom of heaven.*

*Gallery crowds on opening day,
question what his paintings say.
Was his inspiration
the bloody battlefield?
The random streaks of red,
his memories of the war,
of the dead?
Do the bold dark slashes
reflect the Veteran's sorrow;
the bright splashes of yellow,
his hope for tomorrow?*

*Struggling daily with **PTSD**,
he prays his painting
sets him free…*

Words of Gratitude

The Quest

*Matt 13:45—When he found that pearl of great price,
he sold all and bought it.*

*I drove from coast to coast
but I couldn't find it there.
Then I sailed the seven seas
and it still eluded me.
Next, I flew around the world
searching
for that precious pearl.*

*Then I stood still,
and I could see
that all this time,
it was within me!*

Gratitude

Psalm 23:5—My cup runneth over.

Precious memories of my youth:
apple orchards, the community pool,
kitchen aromas after school.
A clean bed to sleep in
three meals a day,
freedom to travel, freedom to pray
By God's loving grace
that was my fate,
deep gratitude!

Alas, the truth in others' youth:
no place to call home, no schools intact,
no bed to sleep in, leftover scraps.
Cities in ruins, complete disarray;
threatened with death, if they dared to pray.
By God's loving grace,
I was spared that fate,
deep gratitude!

Small Town Boys

Eccles 4:10—Pity the man who falls and has no one to pick him up.

"Just running down to the coffee shop,"
Grampa said it every morning,
meeting up with his old pals
in faded ball caps, trading stories;
stayed true friends
throughout the years,
shared their joys, shared their tears.

Retired now, they're close-knit folk,
sharing memories, telling jokes;
closer than a lot of brothers,
feeling blessed
to have each other!
'Small Town Boys.'

Alive, Alive, Oh!

1 Cor.10:31—Whatsoever you do, do all to the glory of God.

Today I thought
I'll just sit
and do nothing...
but then I realized
I was breathing,
and breathing is living;
and living
is "really Something!"

Blessed Am I

Prov.17:6—Children's children: a crown to the aged.

*Today, my baby boy was born,
blessed am I, new mother.
Ten years old, a ball and a glove,
backyard lessons
from his father.*

*Proud as he could be, my son
at his college graduation,
promising me the second dance
at his wedding celebration.*

*Today, his baby boy is born
blessed am I,
Grandmother!*

Gems

*Prov.27:9—Better than incense,
the heartfelt counsel of a friend.*

*A myriad of acquaintances
drifting in and out of our lives;
a procession of beautiful facets,
a profusion of colorful hues
like annual blooms,
often for just one season.
Others,
for whatever reason,
become our lifelong friends.*

*Rare gems;
Treasure them!*

Forever Young

*Lao Tzu—Care what other people think
and you will always be their prisoner.*

*As she frolics in the kiddy pool,
people stare; she doesn't care.
She sees the young mothers
nod to each other:
"She's old and she's odd."*

*Old perhaps,
but odd she's not.
At ninety-one,
still having fun,
living life,
forever young!*

Tomorrow?

*Lao Tzu—The journey of a thousand miles
begins with one step.*

*Far too long since last I paused
to thank God for my blessings.
Tomorrow, I shall do just that;
I'll take some time
to count my blessings...
I'll take some time
tomorrow!*

*Why not today?
Today is mine.
Tomorrow?*

Words of Trust

Let It Be

Psalm 91—My refuge and my fortress;
my God in whom I trust.

There comes a beckoning
from the Stream,
that bids you
cast your inmost dreams
into the flowing course.

Just trust the Stream
to turn your dreams
into reality

Just let it be!

Run, Run, Run

Luke 21:19—In your patience, possess your soul.

Why are we running
at so fast a pace,
so impatient to get
to that other place?
Are our goals that important,
are they really worth the race?

Life will unfold
as it's meant to be!
Why waste so much energy
trying to outrun
the speed of life?

My Collection

Psalm 34:19—The Lord delivers all from their afflictions.

*I filled my basket to the brim
with my worries and my fears;
I'd been collecting them
for years.
I didn't want them anymore.
I rang the bell at heaven's door
and left them there.*

*God accepted with delight.
I slept well that night
without my basket.*

Be Still

Psalm 46:10—Be still and know that I am God!

Another one
of "those days"
when nothing seems
to be going right?

Ease your grip,
just hold the chisel;
let the Lord
wield the hammer!

On Course

Sol—It is your Providence O Father that steers our course.

*Like the ocean liner
beneath sunny skies,
we confidently sail
at top speed.
But come the first storm
like a battered boat,
barely able to keep afloat;
so unsure
where our journey leads.*

*With the Lord at the helm,
let us rest assured,
we'll stay on course
to the Heavenly shores.*

Inspiration

Psalm 83:1—Do not be silent; O Lord, do not be still.

*A closed ear cannot hear
the whispers to the soul…
Often times
'Inspiration'
steals into our silence
in a whisper only.*

Be listening!

Have We Met?

*Shakespeare—This above all, to thine own self be true:
thou canst not then be false to any man.*

*Too often we live
inside a shell,
afraid to show our real self.
Do you think you know me,
know who I am?
Are you a sham, as I am?*

*Time to open mind and heart;
free the fears that keep us apart.
You, no longer living a sham
and I, being who I truly am.
Time to live fully alive;
trusting, loving,
Godly wise.*

Solace

*Psalm 71:5—Thou art my hope O Lord,
my trust from my youth.*

*Why walk the weary road alone?
Keep an ear to hear
the quiet footsteps…
Solace has already begun
the journey to your needs.
In fact, Solace
is standing at your door
just waiting
to be summoned.
Just open the door.*

Maybe

Eccles—There's a time to keep and a time to cast off.

Mother, are you listening?
"Assisted living"
instead of alone
in this big home!

But my memories are here,
all the things I hold dear.
Memories of your dad
and all the joys we had;
but that was yesteryear…

Maybe tomorrow, dear
I'll drop by "Calmful Acres"
to have a chat…
Maybe I'll do that, son.
Maybe…
tomorrow.

Forgiveness

Phil 3:13—Forget what lies behind; press on toward the goal.

*Let us trust that the love, kindness
and service that we've given
are the only deeds that God records
in that golden book in heaven.*

*Time to treat our failures
and those of our friends
with true forgiveness.*

*We tried;
God is satisfied.*

Words of Peace

Utopia

Lao Tzu—Love the world as if it were yourself;
you will then be ready to care for all things.

Would that we could all be blind
to the color of our neighbor's skin.
Better still with eyes wide open,
we could recognize our kin.
And if his house of worship
is a different one from ours,
thank God at least
we both believe
in a higher power.

Only then and not until,
will the world know peace!

Peace

*John 14:27—Let not your hearts be troubled;
my peace I give unto you.*

*With daily worries left aside,
bring no ego, bring no pride
on your journey to your center;
to that sacred place
where "Peace" lies waiting
to be summoned.*

*Despite the daily chaos,
"Peace" can hear your whisper
and Peace cannot resist
an invitation!*

Celebration

Chief Seattle—There is no death; only change of worlds.

*Ninety-five candles on his cake,
the family eager to celebrate.
"I'm an old man for goodness' sake,
keep your party for my wake.
Peacefully strolling
through Heaven's gate;
that's the day I'll celebrate!"*

*No more candles,
no more cake.*

Serenity

Rumi—Silence is the language of God;
all else is poor translation.

City lights left far behind,
country cottage on my mind.
The shimmering lake
in the rise of the moon;
the hauntingly beautiful
trill of the loon.

In silent summer reverie,
God speaks to me:
Serenity!

Hey God!

Omar Khayyam—The thoughtful soul, to solitude returns.

"You have less than a year."
(Words no one wants to hear.)
This can't be true, this must be a lie.
Why me, why me?
I'm not ready to die!
Hey God, are You there?
I want more time;
I want to finish living!
Restless days, sleepless nights;
a real battle to face his plight.
What can I do…
God, what can I do?

Okay God, You win, You win!
If you take good care
of my loving wife, I'll be ready;
take me, tonight.

Downtime

*Muhammad—Contemplation for sixty minutes
is better than worship for sixty years.*

*A race to win, a plan in place,
schedules to keep, deadlines to face.
Never enough hours in the day;
not a moment of peace
amid the fray.
Why do we choose to live this way?*

*How wise the man
who finds time to pray!*

A Better 'Me'

*Gandhi—A man is the product of his thoughts;
what you think, you become.*

*Given the chance to live anew,
would you?
Who would you choose to be?
I'd choose to be 'Me.'
I'd have a blueprint to amend
the wrong choices I made
because I was afraid
of public opinion;
those times I held back
when I should have acted.
All the times I failed
to love.*

*I doubt I'll be given
that second chance;
today I'll get it right, perchance.
Today, I'll be
a better 'Me!'*

Reverie

Psalm 63:6—In the watches of the night,
I meditate on you, O God.

As quiet night embraces me
in peaceful reverie,
I pray to catch a glimpse
of the layered beauty
just beneath
the surface of my soul,
waiting
for discovery.

Words to Ponder

The Carpenter

Psalm 14:1—The fool says in his heart, there is no God.

*The atheist is the first to curse
the God he doesn't believe in,
just because the hammer
came down on his thumb.*

*A carpenter swung the hammer;
the 'Carpenter' made the thumb.
They were bound to meet!*

Chasing the Dream

*Eccles 3:1—For everything there is a season,
a time for every matter under heaven.*

*When she was a little girl,
she couldn't wait to be sixteen
and wear bright red lipstick.
When she was a teenager,
she dreamed of finding
the "love of her life"
and having little babies.
When she was a young mother,
she dreamed of the day
she would be a grandmother.*

*Today, she is a grandmother.
She dreams of being that young mother
who would like to be the teenager who
when she was a little girl,
just wanted to wear
bright red lipstick!*

Temptation

*Lao Tzu—Knowing others is intelligence;
knowing yourself, is wisdom.*

*I never dip my toe
in the pool
if I don't intend to swim.
I can be sure
if the water's warm,
I'll want to jump right in.*

*And once I'm wet,
I'm bound to forget all
my good intentions.*

Poor Rich Man

*Muhammad—It is difficult for a man laden with riches
to climb the steep path to bliss.*

*The chauffeured tycoon
in his private limousine,
custom-made suits, the finest cuisine,
'tis the scene by broad daylight.
A vivid contrast late at night,
in his empty mansion all alone;
his wife and children long since gone.
His principles, he left behind;
his fortune foremost on his mind.*

*Seeking his solace in a bottle of rye,
he sits alone and drinks it dry.
He knows in his heart
he got it wrong.
There is no dance,
there is no song.*

Party Time

Prov.6:20—Children, remember your mother's teaching.

*Teens young and hardy,
the all-night party,
kegs of beer and drugs galore.
Drink up man, have one more!
Staggering out they jump in his car,
"I don't really have to drive that far."*

*Oh God, what was that?
Did my car just crash?
I hear a siren somewhere in my head;
where is my buddy?
Oh God, am I dead?*

*Please Mom, don't cry;
don't ask me why.
I know you warned me,
don't drink if you drive.
Oh God, I'm so sorry;
please don't let me die!*

The Game of Life

Isaiah 55:6—Seek the Lord while He may be found.

Deer tracks in new fallen snow;
hunters aiming, scrunched down low.
Let the game begin!
Shots ring out, they miss their mark;
ammo grazing birch tree bark.
The hunter outwitted
by swift-footed deer;
white tails mocking
here, then there.

Perhaps I need
to check my aim;
change my focus,
change my game...?

Golden Years

Psalm 126:5—Those who sow in tears will reap in joy.

Seniors in their golden years,
freely weep their river of tears.
They cry at weddings
and at the funeral home;
they cry in public, they cry alone.
They cry for joy at the birth of a child;
they cry when you bid them goodbye.
They even cry for strangers who die.
No need to question,
they can't tell you why...

Seniors in their golden years,
freely weep their river of tears.
Just let them be
blissfully free.

The Gate

Matt.7:21—Not everyone who says Lord, Lord, will enter my kingdom.

I worship my God;
it's you I hate.
You, of a different color;
you, of a different faith!

Did I just bolt the gate?

The Sea of Life

Psalm 42:3—Tears have been my food, day and night.

*There'll be tears shed today
and more tears tomorrow;
tears of joy and tears of sorrow.
Tears of gratitude
when a loved one recovers;
tears of relief when one discovers
his illness is curable.
Tears of frustration
to the new paralytic;
tears of helplessness
to be listed as critical.
Tears of joy when a mother learns
her little boy will walk again.*

*There'll be tears shed today
and more tears tomorrow;
the tears that flow
into the Sea of Life.*

Remember?

*Lao Tzu—Only when you realize you have an illness,
can you seek a cure.*

*Whatever happened to the family meal?
Remember how that used to feel?
Father, mother, sisters, brothers,
interested in one another.
Caring, sharing joys and strife;
sharing dinner, sharing life.
'Twas a natural part of every day,
when families came together to pray,
before the days of the P.C.,
iPads, cell phones and direct TV.*

*Whatever happened
to the family meal?
Remember
how that made you feel!*

Drumming

Mark 4: 22—Everything hidden is meant to be revealed.

Forget your native way of life,
forget your language;
learn our rules
in fostered residential schools.
We have come to save your souls!
We, the "men of God."

Stolen years, endless tears;
decades of silence too long kept.
Courage at last to tell the depth
of loss, of pain,
of humiliation, of shame,
all in the "name of God."

Today though free,
still imprisoned by memories.
Never again!
The Empire crumbles;
drum circles rumble
in praise to You,
Gitchi Manitou!

The Answer

*1Cor.2:15—The person with the Spirit
is not subject to merely human judgments.*

*When does life begin?
Theology, psychology,
society, philosophy;
does anyone
know the answer?
If we could ask the unborn fetus,
are we so sure
they'd choose to meet us?
And when life ebbs at ninety-five,
should we decide
our time to die?*

*Does anyone
know the answer?*

Just 'Be There'

*John 15:13—Greater love hath no man,
than he lay down his life for a friend.*

*How often have we said:
"I know how you feel,"
when in fact,
we can scarcely imagine?*

*It's not our heart
that's aching,
nor our world
turned on its end;
it's just our time
to be a friend...
to just
"be there!"*

Reality

Eccles 1—All is Vanity!

*Sometimes it takes a lifetime
to realize that all the energy
we focus on "things,"
adds nothing of value
to our life...
That the "things"
we simply couldn't live without,
are not at all
what life is about.*

*Sometimes
the most beautiful of urns
contain only
ashes...*

Voices of Nature

Awesome!

*Gen 9:13—I have set my bow in the clouds,
as a covenant between Me and the earth.*

*Verdant hillsides,
nature aglow,
swaying cornstalks
row on row.
A summer shower
bids "hello,"
wrapped in ribbons
of a rainbow.*

Awesome!

Spring

Psalm 104:24—The earth is full of Your riches

*Purple crocus peek their heads
along the edge of flower beds;
mother robins gather twigs
to build the baby's nursery.*

*And ducks return
to waiting ponds;
praise the Lord
the winter's gone!*

*Once again,
it's Spring!*

Summer

Psalm 67:6—The land shall yield its increase.

Oh the joy of July!
That first bite
into crimson-peach skin;
rivulets of juices
running down my chin!
Perhaps akin,
intoxicating aroma
of the lilac trees,
chirping chickadees.
A midnight swim,
the moon above;
what's not to love?

A new joy every day;
that's the way
of summer.

Welcome

Psalm 50:11—I know all the birds of the air

Glistening on petals' hue,
early morning dew
waits to greet you.
I sit ever so still,
watch you sip your fill.

With lightning speed
you dart away, to return
a hundred times today;
and every time
you bring a smile.

Welcome,
little hummingbird!
Stay awhile!

Country Lane

*Dalai Lama—The important thing in life,
is to make it meaningful!*

*Brown speckled faces
and silken tresses,
queens in the fields
in our long green dresses;
swaying in the summer sun,
bringing smiles to everyone
who passes by
or chooses to run
barefoot, through our rows
of sunflowers.*

Beside the Sea

Psalm 24:1—The earth belongs to the Lord;
God has founded it on the sea.

The ebb and flow of the tidal shore,
a magnetism I can't ignore;
the scent that hangs in the misty air
soothes my soul when I am there.
No place on earth I'd rather be
than mesmerized beside the sea.

A God-sent blessing
bestowed on me,
born and raised
beside the sea!

R.S.V.P.

*1 Chron. 16:33—The trees of the forest shall sing
for joy before the Lord.*

*On a crisp Autumn day,
stately pines summon the sun
to cast a golden pathway
across their forest floor.*

*To us, they send an invitation
to take a barefoot stroll,
daring us to feel our toes tingle
on the needles
of nature's carpet.*

Say Yes!

Winter Beauty

*Psalm 104:30—Send forth Your spirit O Lord
and You shall renew the face of the earth.*

*Gazing through my window,
the landscape winter white;
the moon and stars my company
in the wee hours of the night.*

*Gazing through my window,
such a calming sight,
glistening new fallen snow,
heavenly delight!*

*Gazing through my window,
unlit homes along the street;
the neighborhood asleep,
missing the thrill
of the winter stillness.*

Mountain Majesty

*Psalm 50:2—Out of the perfection of beauty,
God shines forth.*

*Peaceful giants in your silence,
screaming praise
to God's magnificence!
Water cascading
in endless streams,
where artists and poets
capture their dreams.
Home to the elk,
the deer and the bears;
billions of trees
for billions of years.*

*Ageless, timeless, faithful giants,
we bow
to your Majesty!*

Seasons

*Psalm 74:17—It is You who set the boundaries,
making all seasons.*

*Cold branches laden
with new fallen snow;
barren tress shivering
in the winds of December.
Do they remember
their once beautiful leaves,
now piled like a blanket
at their feet while they sleep?*

*Do they dream
of the summertime,
when once again
the birds will sing
in the green
of their beautiful foliage?*

God's Healing Balm

Lao Tzu—Nature does so much in so little time!

*Blossoming gardens bid us stroll
through vibrant hues of red and gold.
Hula dancing of the willow trees
gently swaying in a summer breeze.
The amazing sight of the tidal bore,
ebbing and flowing along the shore.
A full moon rising across the bay,
announcing the close of another day,*

*Troubles dissolving
in the evening calm...
Nature, truly
God's healing balm!*

Celestial Colors

Gen. 1:31 God saw everything He had made: it was very good.

*God in His heaven,
palette in hand,
creating the colors, as only He can!
The grasses and trees in Spring,
He paints green;
red and amber for Fall,
such a glorious scene!*

*Shades of blue to paint the seas;
waves of white and sea-foam greens.
Golden for the summer days;
silver for the stars at night.
For landscapes in Winter,
He chooses pure white.*

*Then God proclaims,
"I believe I'm done;
enjoy my masterpiece
everyone!"*

Marjorie-isms

Sometimes, a few words speak louder than a tome.

Everyone is entitled to an address.

If you choose to live in the dark, you will never see the light.

Animals talk with their eyes.

Thoughts are words waiting to be born.

Both feet on the ground help you stand firm in your convictions.

If fault is all you can find, stop looking.

Life needs lemons; too much sugar can kill you.

Children should play every day. So should adults.

If you just sit on your hands, you'll miss all life's handouts.

Unconditional love should be a guarantee for every child.

You always have more to give.

Love does not need a reason.

At times, a thought is better left unspoken.

A friend will love you even when you are unlovable.

Less of a good thing is better than more of a bad thing.

You can always find a place for love.

Sometimes, the most beautiful urns contain only ashes.

Eyes belie; the heart, never.

Nature communicates in silence.

Only "you" can do what you do.

Old age trumps youth in memories.
At the seashore, troubles ebb with the tide.

The one that's wrong is usually speaking loudest.

Every vagrant has a soul.

You'll never lift yourself up by putting another down.

The time is always right to apologize.

Only a dog should wag its own tail.

There's always sun behind the cloud.

Inner beauty does not fade with age.

Laugh at yourself; you can be sure others do.

Never say "I will" if you know you won't.

Prudence checks the depth before she dives.

If you don't think you are good enough, be better.

In gratitude, eat everything on your plate (unless it's broccoli).

At times, when you give someone a piece of your mind, it's too much.

I chose a rescue dog; he rescued me.

Want to see a dog smile? Say, car.

Laughter frees clogged arteries.

Be realistic: don't set your goals higher than your ladder will extend.

Ignore any red lights on the road to kindness.

Raise children; never put them down.

The easiest habits to form are the hardest ones to break.

Before you say something you'll regret, press the delete button.

Make sure you understand the problem before you offer the solution.

Nothing on Earth is less fruitful than worry.

Rome would have been built in a day if a busy woman had her say.

Everyday a new song, perfect pitch or off key; keep singing!

Be the towel that dries the river of tears.

Don't run so fast you miss today along the way.

Treat yourself kindly; it's sure to rub off on others.

CPSIA information can be obtained
at www.ICGtesting.com
Printed in the USA
LVHW022251190720
661104LV00017B/987